William the Conqueror

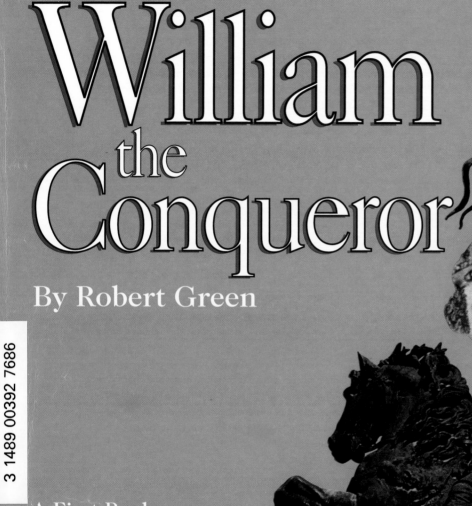

William
the
Conqueror

By Robert Green

A First Book

FranklinWatts

A DIVISION OF GROLIER PUBLISHING

New York   London   Hong Kong   Sydney

Danbury, Connecticut

Photographs ©: Archive Photos: cover, 3, 39 (Popperfoto); Art Resource: 40, 54 (Erich Lessing), back cover, 33 (Giraudon), 34 (Scala); Culver Pictures: cover, 14; E.T. Archive: back cover, 42, 53; New York Public Library Picture Collection: 21; North Wind Picture Archives: 10; Superstock, Inc.: 22, 28, 31 (Musee de la Reine); The Bridgeman Art Library: cover, 7, 15, 19, 26, 37, 43, 46, 51, 13 (Guillaume Cabasson), back cover, 29 (Richard Philp); The Image Works: 27 (Ted Spiegel); Topham Picture Source: cover, 3, 12, 25, 35, 41, 48, 49; UPI/Corbis-Bettmann: 8, 18, 57.

Visit Franklin Watts on the Internet at:
http://publishing.grolier.com

Library of Congress Cataloging-in-Publication Data

Green, Robert, 1969–
William the Conqueror / by Robert Green.

p.   cm.—(A First book)
Includes bibliographical references (p. 58) and index.
Summary: Profiles the Duke of Normandy whose victory at Hastings in 1066 established him as the English king responsible for unifying the system of government and law.
ISBN 0-531-20353-0
1. William I, King of England, 1027 or 8-1087—Juvenile literature. 2. Great Britain—History—William I, 1066-1087—Juvenile literature. 3. Great Britain—Kings and rulers—Biography—Juvenile literature. 4. Nobility—France—Normandy—Biography—Juvenile literature. 5. Military history, Medieval—Juvenile literature. 6. Eleventh century—Juvenile literature. [1. William I, King of England, 1027 or 8-1087. 2. Great Britain—History—William I, 1066-1087. 3. Kings, queens, rulers, etc. 4. Military history, Medieval.]
I. Title.   II. Series.
DA197.G74   1998
941.02′1′092—dc21
[B]   97–10985
                                                                                                      CIP
                                                                                                      AC

Contents

I

THE BASTARD OF NORMANDY

In the autumn of 1064, William, Duke of the French province of Normandy, eyed with hungry eyes the throne of the kingdom of England. His cousin Edward, known as the Confessor, was nearing his last days as king. Edward had no children to succeed him to the English throne. William believed that Edward had promised him the throne, but he could not prove it.

It was during this autumn that the eager Duke of Normandy received some welcome news. Harold Godwinson, Earl of Wessex and one of the most powerful men in England, was shipwrecked on the French coast. William had Harold conducted to the Norman court and greeted the

This fragment of the Bayeux Tapestry shows King Edward, known as Edward the Confessor, lying on his deathbed. The enormous tapestry was woven in 1087 to commemorate the actions of William the Conqueror. It remains an important object for studying the history of this time.

Englishman warmly, a sign of his chivalry—or so it seemed, for a trick lay beneath the courtly gestures.

During Harold's stay in Normandy, William invited Harold on a military campaign against the neighboring French province of Brittany. During the expedition, Harold saved the lives of some Norman soldiers, and William knighted Harold for his bravery. Soon, William began to talk of becoming king of England. He asked Harold for his support and even suggested that Harold

An unhappy Harold touches two shrines while taking an oath of allegiance to William. What Harold did not know is that the shrines hid the relics of saints, giving his oath an unexpected weight.

marry his daughter Adelisa, to show his allegiance. Harold did not give William his enthusiastic support, for the truth was that he, too, was interested in becoming king of England.

Later, at a great ceremony at the castle of Bayeux, William asked Harold to swear an oath of support for his succession to the English throne. Harold once again found himself in an uncomfortable position. To make matters worse for Harold, William had secretly brought bones and relics of Norman saints in two giant boxes into the castle hall, covered them with gold cloths, and asked Harold to swear his oath with one hand on each box. Harold, unwilling to offend William during this solemn ceremony, and not knowing what lay beneath the gold cloths, took his oath. When the cloths were removed and the saints' bones and relics revealed, Harold gasped. An oath taken upon the remains of the dead was sacred.

William's trap had been sprung, and Harold was escorted back to England with a heavy conscience, for he had no intention of supporting William's claim to the English throne. After the death of Edward the Confessor in 1066, William and Harold would discuss the question of succession once again, but this time on the battlefield. The outcome of that great battle, known as the Battle of Hastings, would bring a new reign to England, the dynasty of the Norman conquerors.

The Normans, or Northmen, descended from Viking raiders who had been banished from Norway for piracy in the early tenth century. The exiled Vikings, led by Rolf, their bloodthirsty chief, crossed the icy North Sea in their dragon-prowed ships and landed on the coast of France. The Normans marveled at the richness of the countryside as they sacked city after city; soon, they were on the outskirts of Paris, the capital of France.

The war-loving Viking chief Rolf, also known as
Rollo the Ranger, leads his troops on their conquest
of France. The Vikings had no fear of death,
believing that they would fly directly to the
Viking heaven if they were slain in battle.

The French king, Charles the Simple, besieged in his capital, offered the Vikings the province of Normandy in northwest France to put an end to the raiding. Rolf accepted, and as part of the bargain, he converted to Christianity and was named Duke of Normandy. A most remarkable thing happened after this peace was arranged: The Vikings learned to speak French, became pious Christians, and rebuilt the churches and castles they had destroyed in Normandy.

William, the seventh duke of Normandy, was the direct descendent of Rolf. William's father was Robert the Magnificent, duke before William. Robert had a streak of romanticism that was uncommon in his wily Norman kinsmen. He loved to give away his wealth and venture off on foolhardy escapades, so he was called the Magnificent by his men. The victims of his violent raids, however, nicknamed him Robert the Devil.

One day in 1027, while Robert was riding his horse toward the Norman town of Falaise, he caught sight of a woman washing linen in a stream. Her beauty had a magical effect on the duke. When he discovered that she was Arlette, the daughter of a common tanner, it made no difference to the nobleman. Although already married, Robert carried Arlette to his castle, and in the same year a son, William, was born.

This relief sculpture in Falaise, northern France, shows the meeting of William's parents, Robert and Arlette.

William showed a tenacious resolve even as an infant, and his father was proud of his feisty nature. To the great Norman barons, however, William was something of a joke. He was, after all, the illegitimate son of the daughter of a tanner. Although he would later be known as William the Conqueror, he was known in his own day as William the Bastard.

It was with much astonishment, therefore, that the barons received the news that William was to be named the successor to the dukedom of Normandy in 1034, when he was just seven years old. Robert named a successor because he was departing from his beloved Arlette on a pilgrimage to Jerusalem, the holiest city of Christendom. Robert gathered the nobles of his dukedom and in a solemn ceremony made them swear allegiance to William. "He is but little, my lords," Robert proclaimed, "but he will grow, please God, into a gallant man. I hereby declare him my heir and if I should never return from my pilgrimage you shall accept him as your duke."

Robert then wandered east, where he lived up to his title "the Magnificent" by littering the road to Jerusalem with golden horseshoes and distributing his riches to

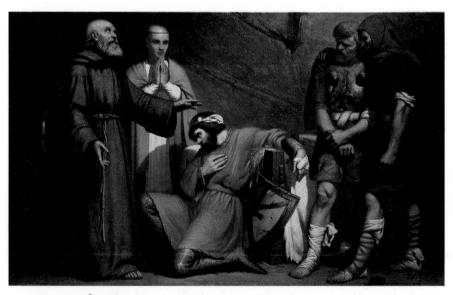

Robert, Duke of Normandy, is blessed by an old monk before setting out on a pilgrimage to Jerusalem—a trip from which he would never return.

King Henry I
of France

the church and to other pilgrims. On the return voyage, Robert fell ill with fever and died. Eight-year-old William was suddenly Duke of Normandy.

The Norman barons, seeing an opportunity to rid themselves of the bastard child, hatched plots to kill William. Three of William's guardians were slain over the next twelve years. One of them was slashed to death in bed while William slept next to him. The assassins had not noticed the child furled in the blankets. When William awoke, he was covered in the blood of his murdered guardian.

Arlette finally decided to hide the child, seeing no other way to protect him. It was a frightful childhood, and one that left a great impression on William's character. In the next ten years, William learned the skills of war and grew into an impressive leader of men.

William grew up to be tall and fair-haired. His wide shoulders reflected his great strength. On his clean-shaven face, he wore a grave and dignified look. When he finally took the battlefield against his many enemies in France, he avenged the deaths of his guardians and showed a ruthless streak that had been nursed in a bloody childhood.

He asserted his right to rule as Duke through war. At age twenty, William joined his liege lord, Henry I, King of France, in a campaign to put down a revolt in the districts of Bessin and Cotentin. In 1047, at Val-ès-Dunes, near Caen, William, carrying a shield emblazoned with two fierce lions, attacked the rebels with King Henry. "Hurling himself upon his enemies he terrified them with slaughter," declared one witness. The rebels were routed.

In 1051, William laid siege to the castle of Alençon, where his enemy Geoffrey Martel, count of

This image of William, whose shield and garments are emblazoned with an English royal lion, is from an illuminated page from the *Liber Legum Antiquorum Regum* (Book of Ancient Royal Law), compiled in the early 1300s.

Anjou, had holed up. At the guardhouse of a key bridge leading to the castle, soldiers taunted William with his low birth. "Hides! Hides! Hides for the tanner!" they shouted. The Normans set fire to the guardhouse, and when the soldiers surrendered, William hacked off the hands and feet of thirty-two soldiers and had them cast over the walls of the castle as a warning. Seeing William's ruthlessness, the castle soon surrendered. William treated his prisoners well, however, and took no revenge on them.

Uprisings continued to occur after this from time to time, but William had succeeded in making himself master of Normandy. He had wrung his right to rule the dukedom from his traitorous noblemen and won the favor of his Norman subjects through his just governance. Having Normandy securely underfoot, William began to look across the English Channel toward the land where his older cousin Edward was king.

II

ENGLAND BEFORE WILLIAM

It may seem strange that William, a French-speaking descendant of Vikings, should believe that he had any claim whatsoever to the throne of England. But one must remember that foreign conquerors and their descendants ruled during much of England's history up to that date.

Julius Caesar, the great Roman general, had glimpsed the Britons in 55 and 54 B.C., only to be driven back

Julius Caesar crossed the English Channel in 55 and 54 B.C., but the fierce Britons beat the Roman expeditionary force back across the channel.

across the English Channel for reinforcements. Roman legions returned and conquered the island. For centuries, they occupied the whole of England. When the Romans withdrew in the early fifth century, the country broke apart into factions and rivalry. Seafaring raiders from northern Germany and from Scandinavia were lured by the natural harbors of the English coast and the fertile fields of England's countryside.

In wave after wave, they landed on the English coast—the Jutes, the Angles (who gave their name to England), the Saxons, the Danes. These invaders slowly moved inland and over time settled into village life. The English throne, however, was a prize for which the different invaders repeatedly fought.

The Anglo-Saxon kings from Wessex—Alfred the Great (king from 871 to 899) and his kinsmen—made headway over the English Danes. But during the reign of Ethelred the Unready (king from 978 to 1016), the Danes again began raiding the English coast, spilling English blood and wending their way to power. The result was the rule of three Danish Kings: Cnut the Great, king of the Danes, Norwegians, and English (king of England from 1016 to 1035); Harold Harefoot, Cnut's illegitimate

Alfred the Great, Saxon king of England, is remembered not only as a strong ruler but also as a scholar who translated important church writings from Latin. This statue of Alfred stands at Winchester Cathedral, Hampshire.

son (king from 1035 to 1040); and Hardecanute, Cnut's son (king of England from 1040 to 1042).

The English throne did not always pass directly from parent to child, as it does today. Instead, the council of wise men, called the Witan, chose or approved the choice of a new monarch. Members of the Witan were drawn from the church and the nobility.

When Hardecanute died in 1042, the Witan declared in favor of Edward the Confessor, forever putting an end to Danish rule in England. The crowning of Edward was considered to be a return to the old English or Saxon dynasty of kings, for his father was Ethelred the Unready. His mother, however, was Emma, the daughter of Richard I, Duke of Normandy. Edward, therefore, was William's cousin.

Edward spent much of his youth in Normandy and spoke French as his first language. He possessed a monkish temperament, and questions of religion appealed to him much more than questions of state. He ordered the construction of Westminster Abbey, where kings and queens of a later age would be crowned. Edward had an elegant bearing and a long bushy beard. But he is remembered above all as being simpleminded and a poor leader of men.

It was necessary for a monarch in the medieval world to exhibit military leadership, which Edward did not pos-

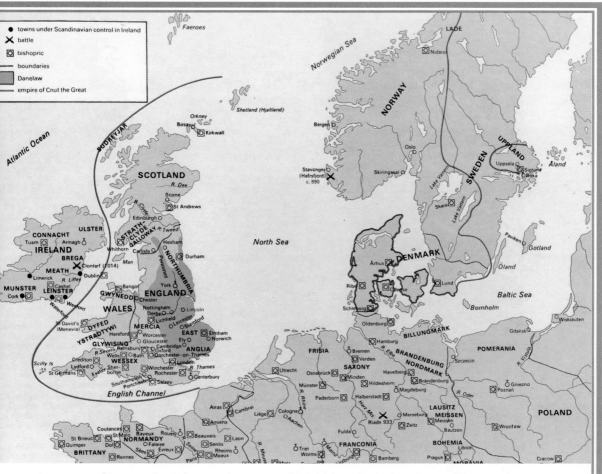

Cnut the Great controlled the lands that are now
England, Scotland, Wales, Denmark, Norway,
and parts of Sweden. Scandinavians who invaded
England during the Anglo-Saxon period had to
make the arduous journey across the North Sea.
Notice how close Normandy is by comparison.

sess. Instead, he relied on William Godwin, the Earl of
Wessex, who had used his influence to make Edward
king. Godwin was the most powerful man in England
during Edward's reign. The blustering and bellicose earl

This painting shows Edward the Confessor taking treasure from his mother, Emma, and pushing her aside. Edward was an impetuous ruler, and later in life he took more interest in the church than the state.

dictated many of the policies of Edward's early reign. Many people believed that Godwin wielded more power than the king himself. But that question was answered in the years 1050 and 1051.

Edward had for some time been filling government posts and religious positions with French-speaking Normans. The truth was that he felt more comfortable surrounded by Normans than Englishmen. Godwin and his followers chaffed at the Norman court. They took up arms in 1050, suffered defeat, and were exiled in 1051. Edward forgave Godwin and his family and invited them to return in 1052, when they resumed almost all of their old influence.

It was during the year 1051 that William visited England. Not much is known of this voyage, except that William was surprised to find that most of the people that he met spoke French and were of Norman descent. One English chronicler wrote, "William Earl came from beyond the sea with mickle company [a large group] of Frenchmen. The king received him and as many of his comrades as seemed to him good and let them go again." When William returned to Normandy, he believed that his heirless cousin Edward had chosen him to be the next king of the English.

When Godwin returned to England, he brought his sons, Harold and Tostig, with him, and the question of succession became acute. William Godwin died, and Harold Godwinson, who inherited his father's earldom of Wessex, wanted the throne for himself, knowing that his was the most powerful family in England. The seeds of war had been sown as the two rivals prepared to assert their claims.

III

PRELUDE TO WAR

pon returning to Normandy, William turned one eye on the ever-restless barons, who were always threatening revolt, and the other eye on a woman named Matilda. William was after a wife, and he chose wisely. Matilda was not only the daughter of the Count of Flanders, a province to the north of Normandy, but she was also related to most of the royal families of Europe. The most illustrious of her ancestors in William's view was Alfred the Great, the Saxon king of England.

William went about his wooing of Matilda in his char-acteristically bold fashion. Matilda met his offer of marriage with utter disgust, claiming that she would rather enter a nunnery than marry the grandson of a tanner. Beneath her contempt lay the fact that she had just fallen in love with another man, a Saxon ambassador from the English court.

William never suffered insults lightly, and according to legend, he rode heatedly to Flanders and thrashed Matilda for her impudence. To everyone's surprise, Matilda then agreed to marry William. When asked why she had changed her mind after such brutal treatment, she replied, "Because I did not know the duke so well then as I do now; for he must be a man of great courage and high daring who would venture to come and beat me in my own father's palace." That was the logic of the medieval mind.

The marriage ceremony took place at Rouen in 1052 and strengthened William's claim to the throne because of his wife's connection with Alfred the Great. The

Matilda of Flanders, William's wife

25

William's subjects considered him to be a fair ruler,
but he was ruthless to those who opposed him.

Catholic Church, however, was not so delighted. Pope Leo IX condemned the union because William and Matilda were cousins. (Nicholas II, a later pope, forgave the couple and sanctioned their marriage. In return, William and Matilda built two abbeys in the Norman town of Caen—St. Stephen's for monks and Holy Trinity for nuns.)

Henry I, King of France and overlord of Duke William, was also alarmed at the marriage of William and Matilda. Through the marriage, William greatly increased his influence in France. Geoffrey Martel, Count of Anjou, the old enemy of William and Henry, joined forces with Henry and invaded Normandy in 1053.

Geoffrey Martel's new alliance with Henry would little have surprised William, who was schooled in war and the treachery of his fellow countrymen. William's cavalry defeated the forces of the king and Martel at the battle of Mortemer. The

This statue of William triumphant on horseback is on display in Falaise, his birthplace.

This scene from the Bayeux Tapestry shows
Edward the Confessor sending Harold
Godwinson on a voyage across the English
Channel to Normandy. It was during this trip
that Harold made his fateful oath to William.

two allies tried again in 1058, when they were turned
back in battle and had their rear guard cut to pieces
while fording a stream. The spoils of victory were the
province of Maine, which was annexed to Normandy, as
well as part of Anjou.

William's ambition had reached a feverish pitch with
all of this success. It was shortly after this victory that the
unfortunate Harold was blown onto the French coast
and found himself the guest of William. Knowing that
Harold was the only other possible successor in England

to Edward's throne, William had reason to be happy with Harold's pledge of support.

When Harold returned to England in 1064, he informed Edward of his promise. The king brooded, realizing that William was taking advantage of Harold. It is even possible that Edward told Harold that he should be the next king. Edward was never a clear-thinking man, and it is partly his fault that the question of succession created so much conflict. Edward probably consoled himself by remembering that the Witan, not he, would actually name the king after all.

Harold also discovered upon his return to England that his brother Tostig was embroiled in a revolt in the north of England. Tostig was the Earl of Northumbria, the northernmost earldom of England. Tostig was growing rich by levying heavy taxes on his subjects. But even worse than that, he spent most of his

King Edward had taken a vow of chastity early in life to demonstrate his devotion to the Church. Even after he was called to the throne by the Witan, he retained his interest in religious matters.

time in the south of England while his henchmen kept order in the north with whip and sword.

Eventually the people of Northumbria revolted, declaring their desire for the Duke of the neighboring earldom of Mercia as their new liege lord. Tostig turned to Harold for troops, but Harold refused, knowing that his brother was an unjust leader. Tostig was exiled to Flanders, where he had married the daughter of the Count, Matilda's sister. He nursed his hatred for Harold.

William must have watched all of this with a keen eye, for Tostig was being forced into sympathy with the Norman cause, or at least with the enemies of Harold. All of this had greatly affected Edward, for he was very fond of Tostig. The king was now over sixty. His beard had turned white and he was quickly fading. He died on January 5, 1066, and was buried in his new abbey at Westminster. The tomb of Edward the Confessor became an attraction for devout Christians, and in 1161, he was made into a saint by the Catholic church.

Edward may have complicated matters by naming Harold as his successor from his deathbed. Upon the Confessor's death, all eyes turned swiftly to the Witan, which proclaimed Harold king of the English. Harold

HIC RE SIDET HAROLD REX AN GLORVM: STIGANT ARCHIEPS

Harold became king of England just two days after Edward's death. The Bayeux Tapestry sought to discredit Harold's rule in part by calling attention to Archbishop Stigand, who was the man who actually crowned Harold and was later condemned for abusing his office.

was crowned the very next day at Westminster Abbey. When William demanded that Harold honor his sacred oath made in 1064, he received no reply. Normandy buzzed with preparations for war.

IV

BATTLE AT THE HOAR APPLE TREE

Harold, now king of England, with not a drop of royal blood in his veins, must not be considered a usurper of the throne. He had proven his leadership in battle and by just governance. For example, he had bowed to the wishes of the Northumbrians by relieving them of his brother's bloodthirsty rule. Also, he came from the most powerful family in England. Above all, he was appointed by the Witan, thereby receiving the sanction of English legal tradition.

The strange flying object woven into the top of the Bayeux Tapestry in this scene is Halley's Comet, which appeared in the early months of 1066. People saw the comet as a sign that Harold's reign was doomed to failure.

It was just that William didn't see it that way, and he settled immediately on plans for an invasion.

William's first concern was to insure that Normandy would not be overrun during his absence. He cajoled or threatened the leaders of neighboring provinces into promising not to attack Normandy. He may even have received the promise of his overlord, the king of France, to respect Normandy's boundaries while he campaigned against England.

He went about raising troops in much the same fashion—through urgings and threats. He added the promise

NAVIGIO:

MARE

William's invasion force included not only men and horses but even a prefabricated wooden castle that was transported across the English Channel and erected on British soil in late September 1066.

that followers would be rewarded with English land or positions in the Norman government should the invasion succeed. In this manner, he raised a force of more than 10,000 soldiers, accompanied by about 3,600 horses, all to be squeezed into 696 ships for the channel crossing.

William then received the blessings of Pope Alexander II for his invasion. In the year 1060, William had been pardoned by the Roman Catholic Church for marrying Matilda. The Catholics saw in William the opportunity to bring the independent-minded English Christians closer to Rome. Pope Alexander II dispatched a special banner, which he had blessed, indicating that William would sail with the support of the Church. He also sent a ring said to be entwined with some of Saint Peter's hair.

While William waited in September 1066 for favorable winds to carry his fleet to England, he learned that a second invasion force had landed in England, that of Harold Hardraade, King of Norway. (His name means "Hard Ruler.") Hardraade had forged an alliance with the exiled Tostig, brother of Harold. Tostig was still smarting from his brother's lack of support and his exile

The Scandinavians continued to be an imposing threat to England. When Harold Hardraade of Norway led an invasion of northern England, Harold Godwinson sped English troops to confront the force. This left William's landing in southern England almost unnoticed.

from Northumbria. He had been looking around Europe for an ally that could help him return to England at the head of an army. He found Hardraade.

Hardraade was one of the great warriors of his time, and he decided to try to seize the English crown for himself. In mid-September, the joint forces of Hardraade and Tostig landed on the Northumbrian coast in the Norwegian's dragon-prowed ships. They quickly defeated the local forces and seized the city of York. Harold marched his forces northward to confront the invaders. Hardraade and Tostig then withdrew to a place seven miles from York known as Stamford Bridge. When Harold and his army reached Stamford Bridge, they caught Hardraade and Tostig off guard.

It was the custom in those days for the opposing commanders to speak before a battle to test the possibility of last-minute negotiations. King Harold met his brother on the field of battle, and a funny conversation took place. Harold offered to return to his brother the earldom of Northumbria in exchange for deserting Hardraade. "And what will you give Harold Hardraade, King of Norway," Tostig called in answer.

"I will give him," replied Harold, "six feet of English earth, or, since he is taller than other men, seven feet of earth, for a grave."

Harold Godwinson's brother Tostig was slain at the Battle of Stamford Bridge. Later, Harold and his remaining brothers lost their lives to the Norman horsemen, as this panel of the Bayeux Tapestry shows.

Tostig stayed with Hardraade, and a bloody battle ensued. After the battle, Hardraade lay dead beneath his war banner, an arrow through his throat, and he was given his seven feet of English earth as promised. Tostig had been cleaved nearly in two by a battle ax, making it difficult to identify the body. When Harold himself finally found his dead brother, he had him buried in York in a solemn ceremony.

Just a few days after the Battle of Stamford Bridge, Harold was celebrating his victory when a messenger rode into the king's camp with alarming news: A Norman force led by Duke William had crossed the English

Channel and landed at the English port of Pevensey.

No one knows if William and Tostig had arranged to invade England at the same time, but there is no doubt that the Battle of Stamford Bridge tilted the scales in William's favor. It appears that fortune smiled on William in other ways, too. The delay in crossing the channel, caused by unfavorable winds, allowed William to land while Harold's forces were tied up in Northumbria. Moreover, the English fleet that had been patrolling the channel for signs of the Norman invasion had just put in for resupply when William made his crossing. This allowed William to land unharassed on the English coast, spotted only after the landing by coastal watchmen.

It was the custom in Saxon England not to retain a professional army, with the exception of the housecarls (the king's household troops). The housecarls were lightly armored mounted soldiers. They did not fight on horseback, but rather used their horses to move them swiftly toward the thick of battle. The rest of the king's army was drawn from shire levies. These were farmers called up by their overlords at times of danger to fight in the area where they lived.

Therefore, when Harold marched southward to meet William, the shire levies for the south of England were already being gathered. Harold probably marched down from Northumbria with only his housecarls.

After wading ashore, William urges
his invasion force to follow him.

The shallow valley running between Telham Hill and Senlac Hill, north of Hastings, is the spot where William's army assembled on October 14, 1066, at 9:00 A.M.

Meanwhile, the Normans set up camp in the countryside around the village of Hastings and waited for Harold's army. The Normans raided the surrounding countryside for food, erected pre-fabricated forts that they had carried from Normandy, and possibly made contact with Normans in southern England who informed William of the movements of the king's army.

On the morning of October 14, 1066, the Norman army advanced on the king's troops, who had just arrived and encamped on Senlac Hill. Contemporary historians say that the forces clashed "near the hoar [ancient] apple tree." Harold's army was most likely greater in number. But William had two distinct advantages. First, he used a body of archers to "soften up" the ranks of his enemies, while the English probably used few archers. Second, William used cavalry, soldiers who actually fought on horseback, unlike the king's housecarls, who dismounted to fight.

At the end of the day the issue was decided. Around the "hoar apple tree" lay the Saxon dead peppered with arrows, cleaved with sword and ax, and speared with

Harold Godwinson perished at the Battle of Hastings after a Norman cavalryman hacked off his leg with a broadsword.

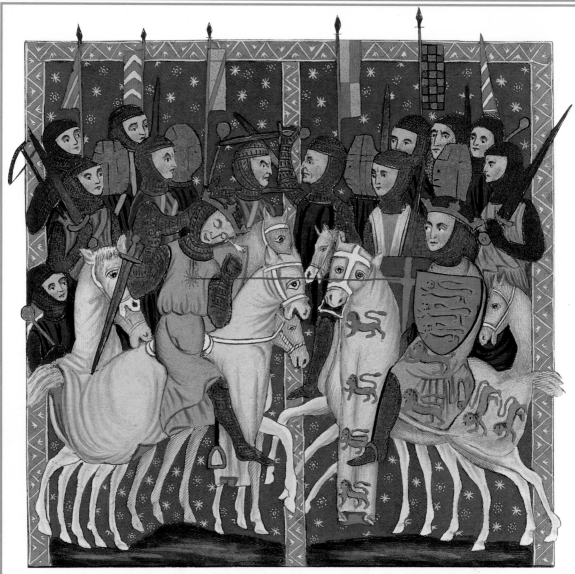

After the battle of Hastings, a legend arose that
William (right) hit Harold (left) directly in the
eye with an arrow. The source of this legend
may have been the Bayeux Tapestry, which
shows a man pulling an arrow from his eye in
the scene depicting the amputation of Harold's leg.

long Norman lances. In the midst of the battle, a Norman soldier named Ivor of Ponthieu, attempting to kill the king and seize his banner, is said to have hacked off Harold's leg. Harold eventually died that day from his wounds. Word of the king's death spread through the ranks, demoralizing all but the housecarls, who fought to the last man, swinging wildly with their war axes.

By day's end, William planted the banner given him by the pope into English soil, kneeled, and gave thanks to God for their victory. When the body of Harold was found, lying under the English standard, William vowed to build an abbey to commemorate his noble foe. The Battle Abbey arose around the spot of the battle in later years, and its high altar still marks the spot of Harold's death.

Harold was buried in stately purple robes in a

The Battle Abbey in Sussex, built by William to house Harold Godwinson's body

plain tomb carved with the words "Harold Infelix" (Harold the Unfortunate). The *Anglo-Saxon Chronicle*, a great source of information on the Norman Conquest, recorded that Harold the Unfortunate "met little quiet as long as he ruled the realm."

Having won the battle of Hastings, William was free to march on London. The city, fearful of his advance, threw open its gates, and on Christmas day in 1066, he was crowned William I, King of the English, at Westminster Abbey.

V

THE CONQUEROR'S LEGACY

After his coronation, William wondered at his own success. Had he really conquered England by victory in a single battle? He wisely seized the castle at Dover, a southern port city, to ensure resupply from Normandy and then set about driving resistance out of the rest of southern England. The resistance lingered, but the fact was that no one seriously challenged his claim to the throne. Even when the Witan

The coronation of William is shown in this illumi-
nated manuscript page from the *Anciennes
Chroniques d'Angleterre* (History of Ancient
England), compiled in the 1400s.

announced that it was supporting Edgar Atheling, the last remaining relative of the West-Saxon dynasty, the claim was swept aside by Norman troops.

In 1067, William returned to Normandy to celebrate his victory and make sure all was well in the dukedom, which was being ruled by his wife Matilda. William left the English government in the hands of his half-brother Odo, Bishop of Bayeux. Odo ruled without William's sense of justice, and revolts quickly arose in the north, south, and west of England, forcing William to return quickly from Normandy.

The personal leadership of William was necessary to rule the English. It is a tribute to his greatness that William tempered his military victories with wise decisions about how to govern his English prize.

As William subdued England, he distributed feudal fiefs—estates where lords loyal to the king held sway—to his Norman knights. This upset the traditional power of the followers of Harold and all the old English families. To control the English, the Normans dotted the country with castles. At first these castles were nothing more than wooden defense positions. Later, stone was quarried and elaborate walled structures arose. Many of these castles can still be seen today.

William held the Norman barons planted in these new castles responsible for keeping peace in the region.

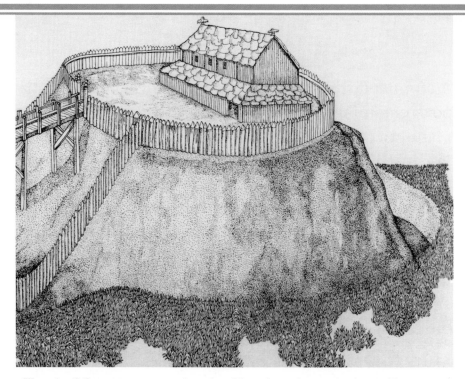

Early Norman castles in England were hastily constructed of wood, but they were very secure. As this drawing shows, moats and strong fences protected the Normans from possible English rebellion.

He dissolved the great earldoms such as Northumbria and Wessex, insuring that power revolved around the king in London. With more power at his command, William imported the Norman feudal system to England. The English, who for so long had been loyal primarily to local chiefs, were brought under a central government.

Local sheriffs, however, who were responsible for law and order at the village level, were left in place. People agreed that this was a just act by the new government, for not even the Normans were above the legal powers of the local sheriffs.

Although the Saxon peasants bristled at the high taxation levied by William, they considered him a fair king and soon accepted him as the rightful heir to the English throne. He won them over in part with his personal charisma. Part of the secret of this success was

The Normans erected stone castles to house the nobility who controlled the new feudal system, by which they controlled the local population. Berkeley Castle in Gloucester, built in 1153, is the second oldest inhabited English castle (after Windsor).

the fact that England had never really been a unified country. Power was divided, and local wars were common. The Norman administration introduced a peace in the country not really known before. Above all, they gave the people of England—Norman and Saxon alike—a feeling that England was a united kingdom.

It must be said, however, that William and many of his Norman followers still considered Normandy their home. William never renounced his claims to Normandy after the conquest of England. For a time, the two were governed together.

Wales and Scotland—which together with England form Britain—remained separate kingdoms. At various times both the Welsh and the Scots supported revolts against William. The Scots went so far as to declare in favor of Edgar Atheling for the throne. In 1072, William marched his Norman knights northward, defeated the Scots, and received the pledge of the Scottish king, Malcolm, to be a loyal vassal of the English king. The Welsh were similarly quelled by force. From that time forward, little was heard about general rebellions against the Normans.

The Normans helped lay the foundations of the English government and legal system. An equally lasting mark of Norman rule in England can be found on the English language. The Normans introduced into the

This page from the *Historia Anglorum* (History of England), compiled in the 1200s, shows William the Conqueror (upper left) and the three kings who succeeded him: William II, Henry I, and Stephen. Each monarch holds a model of a cathedral in his hand, to represent their commitment to the continuation of Christian rule in England.

Saxon (old English) tongue a wealth of words from French and from Latin, the parent language of French. Modern English is the direct result of this mingling of languages.

Through their French-speaking conquerors, the English were also brought into the European fold. That is to say that their national identity began to move away from their Scandinavian ancestry and toward the rest of continental Europe. The result—though the English have always remained independent-minded—was to introduce many new European ideas to England.

In 1085, William commissioned the *Domesday Book* to record the distribution of land among the Norman barons. Since that time, many of the richest and oldest families of England have taken pride in finding their ancestors among its pages.

Another great source of information about Norman England is the Bayeux Tapestry. The 230-foot tapestry was commissioned shortly after the Battle of Hastings to celebrate the Norman victory. It was possibly created under the direction of Odo, Bishop of Bayeux. It is woven in embroidery in brilliantly colored strands of wool. The tapestry gives us the most reliable account of what William, Harold, Odo, Edward, and others looked like. It also gives clues to battle dress, weapons, ships, and

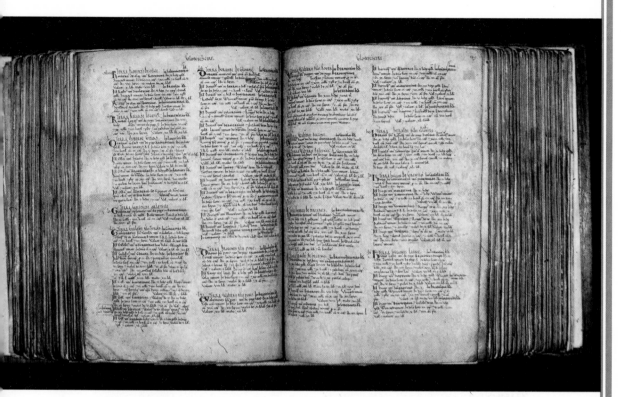

The *Domesday Book* listed the possessions of nobles in England in remarkable detail. These pages show the land holdings of residents in Gloucestershire.

other specifics of the day.

The Bayeux Tapestry is essentially a work of propaganda, not only advertising the Norman victory at Hastings but also stressing the legal claims that William had to the English throne. The tapestry has always resided in France at the Cathedral of Bayeux. One strange exam-

ple of the tapestry's usefulness occurred in the 1940s. During World War II (1939–1945), the Nazis inspected the Bayeux Tapestry on a number of occasions to find clues to how Germany could successfully invade England. They failed, however, and not since the Norman Conquest has anyone invaded the British Isles.

In 1087, William was again in Normandy. Treacherous and greedy neighbors threatened the dukedom again. The Normans under William's command leveled and set fire to an enemy town to punish the citizens for rebelling. William rode out to see the destruction, and it was then that a most unfortunate thing happened. His horse lost its footing, and William was thrown into a ditch smoldering with hot embers. He was carried to the town of Rouen in great pain. The fall proved to be fatal—the conqueror died on September 9, 1087. He was buried as he wished in Normandy and his body enshrined at Saint Stephen's in Caen.

The spot of his burial is still marked in his abbey, but his bones and relics were scattered by Huguenots

The Bayeux Tapestry tells the story of the Battle of Hastings through pictures, much as a book does in words. This closeup shows William remounting after being unhorsed in the battle. He is showing his face to his men to dispel the rumor that he had been slain in battle. William, unlike military commanders today, personally led his troops into battle. Reports of the death of their commander could quickly demoralize an army.

(French Protestants) in 1662. The tomb was further desecrated in 1793 by French Revolutionaries. Yet William has never been forgotten. He is too much responsible for the shaping of England, bringing to it unity and law. "He was a very stern and violent man," it is recorded in the *Anglo-Saxon Chronicle* of 1087, "so that no one dared do anything contrary to his will. . . . Amongst other things the good security he made in this country is not to be forgotten."

In the middle of William's funeral service, a churlish Englishman interrupted to claim that he owned the very land where the king was to be laid to rest and that he hadn't been paid properly for it. Someone paid him what he wanted and the solemn ceremony continued.

For More Information

Luckock, Elizabeth. *William the Conqueror*. New York: G. P. Putnam's Sons, 1964.

Martell, Hazel M. *Normans*. New York: Macmillan Books for Young Readers, 1992.

Sauvain, Philip. *Hastings*. New York: New Discovery (Macmillan), 1992.

Williamson, David. *Debrett's Kings and Queens of Britain*. Topsfield, Mass: Salem House Publishers, 1986.

For Advanced Readers

Barclay, Brigadier C. N. *Battle 1066*. Princeton, N.J.: Nostrand Company, 1966.

Cannon, John, and Ralph Griffiths. *The Oxford Illustrated History of the British Monarchy*. New York: Oxford University Press, 1989.

Churchill, Winston. *History of the English Speaking Peoples*. New York: Dodd, Mead & Co., 1956.

Lloyd, Alan. *The Making of the King: 1066*. New York: Holt, Rinehart and Winston, 1966.

Internet Sites

Due to the changeable nature of the Internet, sites appear and disappear very quickly. Internet addresses must be entered with capital and lowercase letters exactly as they appear.

The Yahoo directory of the World Wide Web is an excellent place to find Internet sites on any topic. The directory is located at:

http://www.yahoo.com

Many Web sites and search engines provide information and links on broader topics in history. One example is a Web page called History Resources, a guide to a huge variety of history sites:

http://www.liv.ac.uk/~evansjon/humanities/history/history.html

You can use search engines and pages of links to find many, many Internet sites about medieval history, art, culture, people, and more. Two examples of resources on-line are a site that shows reproductions of every section of the Bayeux Tapestry:

http://blah.bsuvc.bsu.edu/bt

and Brittania's Battle of Hastings Homepage, a lively site with details about the Bayeux Tapestry and the Domesday Book as well as William I, the Battle of Hastings, the impact of the Norman Invasion on society, and battle reenactments:

http://www.dmcl.com/1066ad/hastings.htm

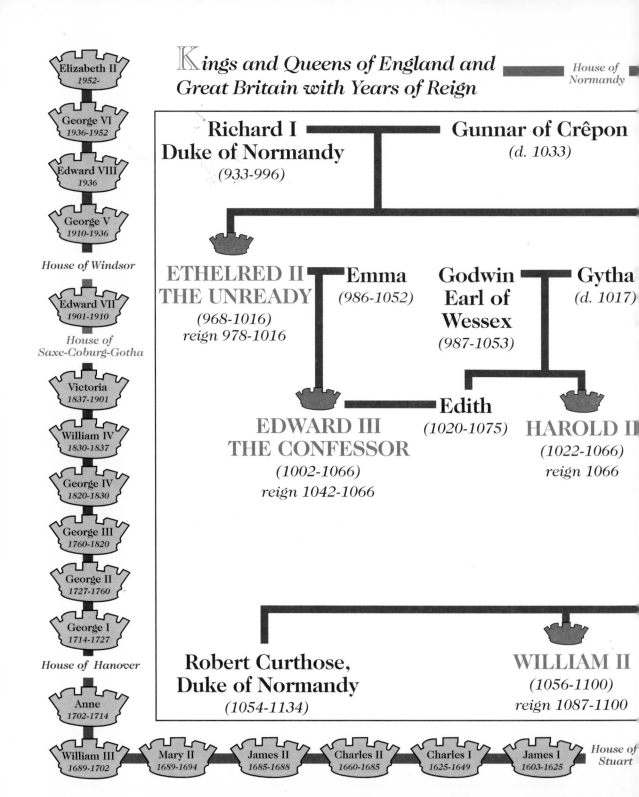

Kings and Queens of England and Great Britain with Years of Reign

House of Normandy

House of Windsor

Elizabeth II
1952-

George VI
1936-1952

Edward VIII
1936

George V
1910-1936

House of Saxe-Coburg-Gotha

Edward VII
1901-1910

Victoria
1837-1901

William IV
1830-1837

George IV
1820-1830

George III
1760-1820

George II
1727-1760

George I
1714-1727

House of Hanover

Anne
1702-1714

William III
1689-1702

Mary II
1689-1694

James II
1685-1688

Charles II
1660-1685

Charles I
1625-1649

James I
1603-1625

House of Stuart

Richard I Duke of Normandy
(933-996)

Gunnar of Crêpon
(d. 1033)

ETHELRED II THE UNREADY
(968-1016)
reign 978-1016

Emma
(986-1052)

Godwin Earl of Wessex
(987-1053)

Gytha
(d. 1017)

EDWARD III THE CONFESSOR
(1002-1066)
reign 1042-1066

Edith
(1020-1075)

HAROLD II
(1022-1066)
reign 1066

Robert Curthose, Duke of Normandy
(1054-1134)

WILLIAM II
(1056-1100)
reign 1087-1100

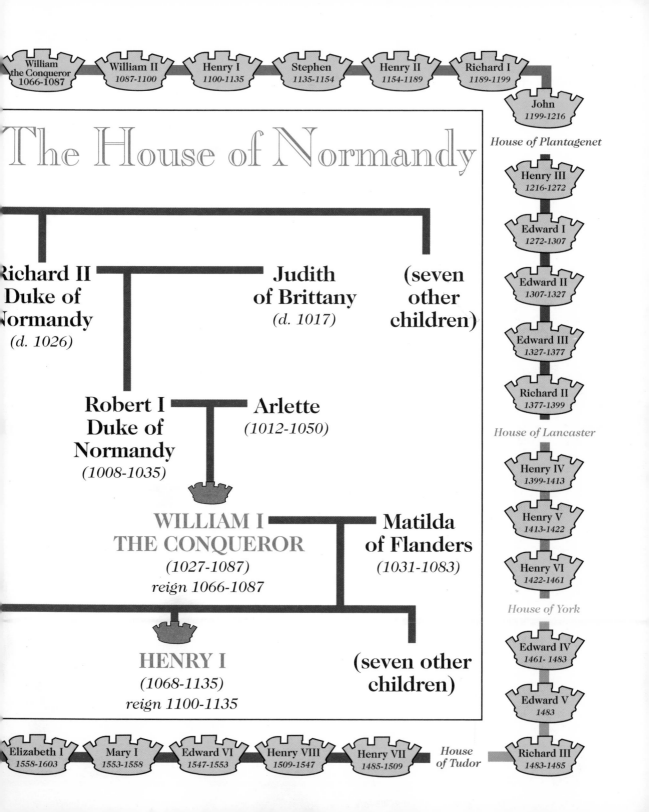

The House of Normandy

William the Conqueror
1066-1087

William II
1087-1100

Henry I
1100-1135

Stephen
1135-1154

Henry II
1154-1189

Richard I
1189-1199

John
1199-1216

House of Plantagenet

Henry III
1216-1272

Edward I
1272-1307

Edward II
1307-1327

Edward III
1327-1377

Richard II
1377-1399

House of Lancaster

Henry IV
1399-1413

Henry V
1413-1422

Henry VI
1422-1461

House of York

Edward IV
1461-1483

Edward V
1483

Richard III
1483-1485

House of Tudor

Henry VII
1485-1509

Henry VIII
1509-1547

Edward VI
1547-1553

Mary I
1553-1558

Elizabeth I
1558-1603

Richard II Duke of Normandy *(d. 1026)*

Judith of Brittany *(d. 1017)*

(seven other children)

Robert I Duke of Normandy *(1008-1035)*

Arlette *(1012-1050)*

WILLIAM I THE CONQUEROR *(1027-1087) reign 1066-1087*

Matilda of Flanders *(1031-1083)*

HENRY I *(1068-1135) reign 1100-1135*

(seven other children)

Index

Page numbers in *italics* refer to illustrations.

Robert Green is a freelance writer who lives in New York City. He is the author of *"Vive la France": The French Resistance during World War II* and biographies of important figures of the ancient world: *Alexander the Great, Cleopatra, Hannibal, Herod the Great, Julius Caesar,* and *Tutankhamun,* all for Franklin Watts. He is also the author of biographies of other British monarchs: *Queen Elizabeth I, Queen Elizabeth II, King George III, King Henry VIII, and Queen Victoria.*